better together*

*This book is best read together, grownup and kid.

a kids
book
about

a kids book about

DESiGN

by Jason Mayden

a
kids
book
about

Printed in the United States of America.

A Kids Book About books are available online: *akidsco.com*

To share your stories, ask questions, or inquire about bulk purchases (schools, libraries, and nonprofits), please use the following email address: *hello@akidsco.com*

ISBN: 978-1-953955-62-3

Designed by Jason Mayden
Edited by Jelani Memory

For Khalil, Viviana, Shani,
Saniyah, Albert, and Donnell.

Dream BIG kids.

Love, Dad / Uncle Jason

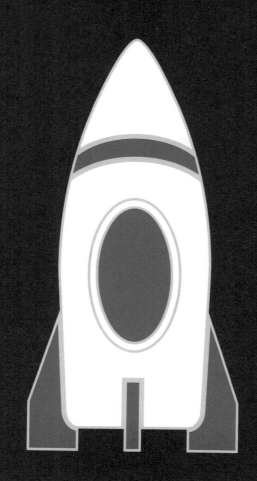

Intro

Over the past 20 years, I have traveled the globe learning, practicing, and teaching about the power of design. I have come to understand that design is an intention, a way of seeing and engaging with the world around you. Design is a desire to make things better and when done well, it is indistinguishable from magic.

As society continues to evolve, we must encourage our youth to ask deeper questions which lead to more equitable solutions. Design is not just a vocation nor is it solely based on artistic ability. It requires the practitioner to immerse themselves in the lives of those they intend to serve. It is an act of empathy that lies at the intersection of emotional intelligence and creativity.

While reading this book with your aspiring designer, I want you to remain curious, to explore your ideas in both visual and physical form, and to experience the world around you with a beginner's mindset. The process of design is a wondrous adventure. I am so excited you have chosen to get started today!

Remember to be playful, be willing to fail, and do everything with honor and gratitude.

This is the way.

You're probably wondering...

what is DESiGN?

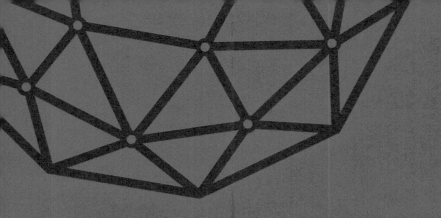

Maybe you think it's things like...

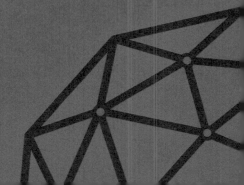

making a cool app,

drawing an amazing building,

or creating a pair of fly sneakers.

But design isn't just those things—

it's so much more!

Design is

1. Asking the **biggest** questions.

2. Having **empathy** for other people.

3. Being **curious** about the world around you.

4. Living out **creative compassion** daily.

Design isn't just
what I do for my job.

It's a lifestyle.

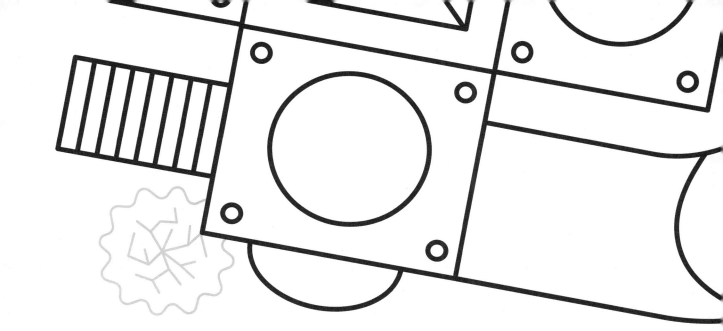

My name is Jason,
and I'm a designer, an educator,
an entrepreneur, and a dad.

When I was a kid, I had a severe infection called septicemia.*

*Septicemia is an infection in your blood.

It was really dangerous.

I was only 7 years old,
and it was likely I would die.*

*It was super scary at the time, but thankfully,
I got better and am here now to tell you this story.

In my hospital bed,
all I could do was read
and use my

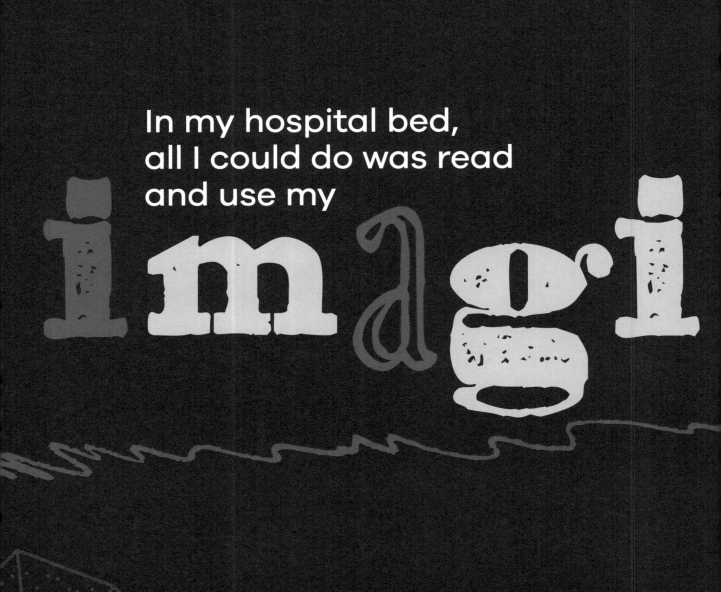
imagi

Nation.

So I dove into comic books all day.

Batman was one of my favorites.

One day, in the comic I was reading, Batman was talking to a man who looked just like me...

Dr. Lucius Fox! A Black designer, creator, inventor, and CEO of Wayne Enterprises who was responsible for making all of Batman's gadgets.

Pretty cool, huh?!

I knew then that when I grew up, I wanted to be just like **Dr. Lucius Fox**— I wanted to invent for my heroes.

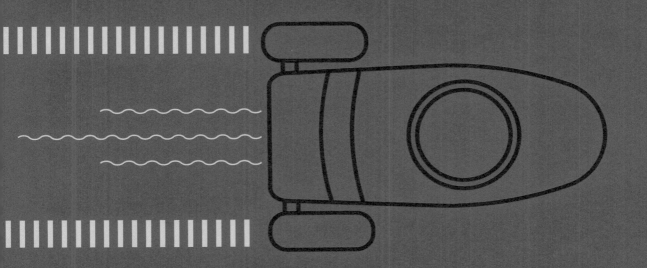

When I was a kid, the closest thing to a hero like Batman was **Michael Jordan**—MJ!

I wanted to build gadgets for him.

But I didn't know where to start.

So I began by asking
questions like

HOW, WHERE, wHO, wHaT, AND wHY?

And I sketched my ideas
on every kind of paper,
from notebooks to napkins...

and I visited all kinds of museums
to learn and find inspiration!

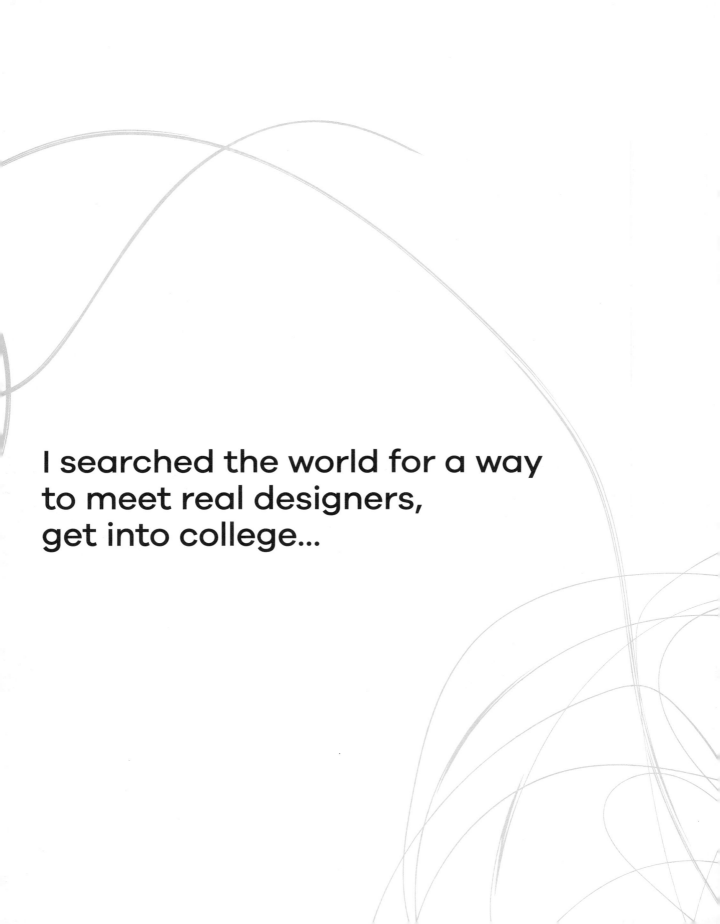

I searched the world for a way
to meet real designers,
get into college...

and eventually find a way
to Nike (the company where
MJ's gadgets came from).

And just like many superheroes,
I faced failure—a lot.

BUT I PERSEVERED.

Each time I was rejected, I learned something new about myself and I became a better designer.

Eventually, I achieved my dream of becoming Nike's first Black industrial design intern.

More specifically, I was Jordan brand's first design intern.

My dream of becoming the gadget designer for a real-life superhero came true!

I have since gone on to design lots of products, experiences, and even companies in my time as a designer.

And along my journey,
here's what I've learned.

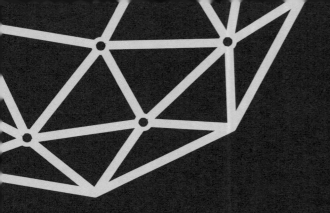

There's more than one kind
of designer and a lot of people
you may not think of as designers.

Here's a few of them:

- Story designers like journalists and filmmakers.

- Financial designers like business owners and investors.

- Wellness designers like counselors and therapists.

- Education designers like teachers and mentors.

- Image designers like barbers, hair stylists, and photographers.

- Policy designers like politicians, city council members, and civil servants.

- World designers like urban planners and civil engineers.

- Industrial designers like me!

All of these people design
in their own way, using creativity
and compassion to solve problems,
make things, and create
for the better.

And there are even more kinds of designers yet to be imagined—

maybe even by You!

One thing I've learned in my journey as a designer is that...

design has to be INCLUSIVE and reflect the WHOLE WORLD AROUND US.

Making design inclusive means that while every problem may not be one you experience, all problems deserve a good solution.

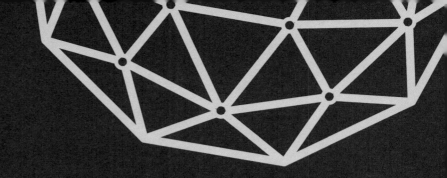

They may be problems
someone else feels
or goes through.

And those people may
look different than you.

They may sound
different than you too.

And they may live
in a completely different
part of the world than you.

Inclusive design recognizes
that differences are beautiful and
allows designers to create for...

EVERYONE.

Every person deserves access
to things that are designed well.

Not just sneakers or cars,
but also homes, communities,
water sources, and food.

Do you want to make something that impacts someone else, builds a community, and changes the world?

Well, it takes a process.

Here are the 9 steps I use:

Step 1:
HAVE EMPATHY.

You have to care for others who are
different from you. Starting here
allows you to understand the person
or community you are designing for.

Step 2: CHALLENGE YOUR ASSUMPTIONS.

Everyone has biases,* but that doesn't mean the way you think works for everybody (or that it's the only right way!).

By challenging your assumptions about people and how the world works, you learn a lot about what you don't know.

*Having biases means believing that some people or things are better than others, which usually results in treating people unfairly.

Step 3: HAVE A BEGINNER'S MINDSET.

With a new skill, everybody starts from square one.

Ask lots of questions, use curiosity like a superpower, and rely on those who have more experience to help you truly understand what design needs are out there.

OBSERVE.

Learn from and with the folks you're designing for.

Listen with open eyes, ears, and mind so that you can understand what they need and what problems you're solving.

Step 5:
ENGAGE.

This is the fun part!

Sketch, talk, prototype,* create, all to discover THE IDEA.

Begin to play with color, materials, and shape to find the solution that is going to work.

*A prototype is a first draft of a new product.

Step 6:
EDUCATE.

Does your designed solution fix the problem you set out to solve?

Remember, feedback is a gift from the people who are working with you.

Be humble and take it in—they're here to support you in your goals and have your best interest at heart!

Step 7:

REFINEMENT.

Edit based on feedback
and trial-and-error, and maybe
simplify your process.

This can often reveal the simplest
solution, bringing you one step
closer to solving the problem
you are trying to tackle.

Step 8:
LAUNCH.

Your design is finished!

Get it out into the world
and in peoples' hands.

Listen and learn how it's received
and get feedback on the impact
it's having—or not having.

Step 9:
SUSTAIN.

Spoiler alert: the design process does not end with launch.

Great designers remain curious about how their design is impacting the world.

The goal is to keep learning and create newer, better solutions in the future.

Once you finish step 9,
it leads you right back
to step 1 all over again.

They just keep going
in a big circle!

Now, we've covered a lot
of important stuff together.

But the **MOST** important thing I want you to remember about **GOOD** design is that it should make things better.

Better

Better for

Better for

for you.
Your community.
the world.

And believe it or not,
you already know a lot
about how to do this.

When you play, pretend, make believe, and dream, you are using your creative self and intelligence to design something that doesn't exist.

So go play...

and DESIGN a better tomorrow, TODAY.

Sketch Your ideas.

Outro

Now that you've learned about the process of design, how do you feel? Inspired, excited, more creative, more confused? The design process takes you through a range of emotions. It challenges your assumptions and biases. It pushes you toward immersive empathy.

My hope is you now feel more empowered to pursue your creative aspirations regardless of age, gender, socioeconomic status, religion, physical ability, or ethnicity.

Design is ever-changing. It consistently requires new ways of thinking AND doing. Design always needs YOU. Your voice and your ideas are valid and important. You have the power to change the world around you for the better.

As you reenter the world, you now have fresh eyes to see and ears to hear. You are more equipped to challenge convention and create the unimaginable.

You have the power. Now the question is...how will you use it for the betterment of your family, your school, your community, and the world?

I can't wait to see what you design!

find
more
kids
books
about

creativity, community, failure, empathy, identity, optimism, imagination, mindfulness, gratitude, adventure, and self-love.

share your read*

*Tell somebody, post a photo, or give this book away to share what you care about.

 @akidsco